U1032813

CHAIM WEIZMANN

The second Herbert Samuel Lecture
delivered on 19th November, 1957,
under the auspices of the
British Friends of the Hebrew University of Jerusalem

CHAIM WEIZMANN

BY

ISAIAH BERLIN

FARRAR, STRAUS and CUDAHY
NEW YORK

Copyright © 1958 by ISAIAH BERLIN

PRINTED IN GREAT BRITAIN BY
THE SHENVAL PRESS LTD
LONDON, HERTFORD AND HARLOW

CHAIM WEIZMANN

I

I SHOULD like to begin by thanking the English Friends of the Hebrew University of Jerusalem for inviting me to deliver this year's Herbert Samuel Lecture.[1] The very title of it plainly demanded a large theme, worthy of the eminent British statesman who has demonstrated by his own devoted and upright life the baselessness of all the charges brought against the Jews of an inescapable double allegiance. He has done us all the unique honour of presiding over this occasion of which he is the eponymous hero; and I can conceive of no subject that is more worthy of him than the personality and outlook of a man bound to him by ties of a long political and personal friendship, and by a cause that, even when they disagreed most deeply, dominated both their lives. This man is Dr Chaim Weizmann. His achievement—and the details of his public life—are too fresh in our memories to need description or analysis from me. His personal characteris-

[1] A portion of this lecture was incorporated in the Weizmann Memorial Lecture which the Zionist Council of the city of Leeds invited me to deliver in February 1958. I should like to thank this body for kindly permitting me to reproduce it here.

tics are less well known. He was the only statesman of genius whom I have ever had the good fortune of knowing intimately, and I am grateful for the opportunity of trying to convey something of its quality. Something: no more than a small part of a character and a life unique in our time.

To know—to enjoy the friendship of—a great man must permanently transform one's ideas of what human beings can be or do. Social theorists of various schools sometimes try to convince us that the concept of greatness is a romantic illusion—a vulgar notion exploited by politicians or propagandists, and one which a deeper study of the facts will always dispel. There is no way of finally refuting this deflationary theory save by coming face to face with an authentic instance of greatness and its works. Greatness is not a specifically moral attribute. It is not one of the private virtues. It does not belong to the realm of personal relations. A great man need not be morally good, or upright, or kind, or sensitive, or delightful, or possess artistic or scientific talent. To call someone a great man is to claim that he has intentionally taken (or perhaps could have taken) a large step, one far beyond the normal capacities of men, in satisfying, or materially affecting, central human interests. A great thinker or artist (and by this I do not necessarily mean a man of genius) must, to deserve this title, advance a society, to an exceptional degree, towards some intellectual or aesthetic goal, for which it is already, in some sense, groping; or else alter its ways of thinking or feeling to a degree that would not, until he had performed his task, have been conceived as being within the powers of a single individual. Sometimes such an achievement is felt as a great act of liberation by those upon whom such a man binds his spell, sometimes as an enslavement, sometimes as a peculiar mixture or succession of both. Similarly, in the realm of action, the great man seems able, almost alone and single handed, to transform one form of life into another; or—what in the end comes to the same—permanently and radically alters the outlook and values of a significant body of human beings. The transformation he effects, if he is truly to deserve his title, must be such as those best qualified to judge consider to be antecedently improbable—something unlikely to be brought about by the mere force of events, by the 'trends' or 'tendencies' already working at the time—that is to say, something unlikely to occur without the intervention, difficult or impossible to discount in advance, of the man who for this very reason deserves to be described as great. At any rate that is how the situation will look in retrospect. Whether this is a vast mistake—whether, in fact, human beings (as Marx, or Tolstoy, for instance, believed) overestimate

the importance of some of their own number
—whether some more impersonal view of history, that does not admit the possibility of
heroes, is in fact correct, cannot be discussed here. If the notion of the hero who
makes or breaks a nation's life springs from
an illusion, it is, despite all the weighty argu-
ments produced against it, a very persistent,
obsessive and universal illusion, to which the
experience of our own time has given powerful support. At any rate, with your permis-
sion, I propose, for the purpose of this address,
to assume that it is not delusive, but a true
view of society and history. And thence I
should only like to embark on the compara-
tively modest proposition, that if great men—
heroes—have ever existed, and more particularly if individuals can in any sense be said
to be the authors of revolutions that permanently and deeply alter many human lives—
then Dr Chaim Weizmann was, in the sense
which I have tried to explain, a man of this
order.

I have said that one of the distinguishing
characteristics of a great man is that his active
intervention makes what seemed highly improbable in fact happen. It is surely difficult
to deny that the actions which culminated in
the creation of the state of Israel were of this
improbable or surprising kind. When Theodor Herzl began to preach that it was both
desirable and possible to set up a sovereign

Jewish state of a modern type by means of a formal, public act of recognition by the great powers, most sane, sensible, reasonable people, both Jews and Gentiles, who heard of this plan, regarded it as quite insane. Indeed, it is difficult to see how they could have thought otherwise. In the nineteenth century the Jews presented an exceedingly anomalous spectacle. Scattered among the nations of the world, they constituted something which it was hard or perhaps impossible to define in terms of such concepts as nation, race, association, religion or the other terms in which coherent groups of a hereditary or traditional type were commonly described. The Jews were clearly not a nation in any normal sense of the word: they occupied no fixed territory of which they constituted the majority of the population; they could not even be described as a minority in the sense in which the ethnic or national minorities of multi-national empires—the Austro-Hungarian, or Russian, or British Empires were so denoted—they occupied no stretch of country which could be called their native territory in the sense in which Welshmen, or Slovaks, or Ruthenians, or Zulus, or Tartars, or even Red Indians or Australian aborigines—compact continuous groups living on their ancestral soil—patently did so. The Jews certainly had a religion of their own, although a good many of them did not appear to profess it in any clearly recognizable sense; but they could not be defined as a solely religious body; when in modern times Jews were discriminated against or persecuted, it was, for the most part, not their religious observances that were in the first place abhorred; when Jews who had left their faith and had become converted to Christianity—like Disraeli or Karl Marx or Heine —were thought of, the fact that they were still looked upon as Jews, or as being of Jewish origin, certainly did not imply merely that their ancestors had practised a religion different from that of the surrounding populations. Nobody, after all, spoke of persons of Presbyterian, or Roman Catholic, or even Moslem origin or descent; a man might be of Turkish or Indian origin—but hardly of Moslem descent or of Moslem race. What, then, were the Jews? Were they a race? The word 'race' was, and is still, felt to carry somewhat disreputable associations. Vague historical notions such as those of Indo-European or Mongol race were at times used by ethnologists. Groups of languages were occasionally classified as Aryan or Hamitic or Semitic, but these were at most technical terms for defining the culture of those who spoke them. The idea of race as a political description was not, towards the end of the last century, one which intellectually respectable persons held with; it was felt to be connected with the undesirable attitudes of national or cultural chauvinism. Indeed it was its lurid propagandist colour that made the word itself, whatever its context, seem a strong appeal to prejudice. Competent ethnologists, anthropologists and sociologists vied with each other in proving that there were no 'pure' races, that the notion was hopelessly vague and confused. But if the Jews were not a race, what were they? A culture, or 'way of life'? Apart from the fact that they participated, at any rate in the countries of the West, in the civilization of their surroundings, this seemed a very thin notion in terms of which to define something so immediately recognizable, a group of persons towards whom feelings were as strong and definite as they quite clearly were in respect of the Jews. For there undoubtedly existed certain cardinal differences in outlook and behaviour, and to a large degree in outward physical characteristics, that appeared to be persistent, hereditary and easily recognizable both by the Jews themselves and by non-Jews. So much seemed clear to any honest man who was not either too embarrassed or too polite to face the obvious facts. The martyrdom of the Jews in the Christian world was so painful and notorious, the wounds which it had inflicted on both persecutors and persecuted were so deep, that there was a natural temptation on the part of enlightened and civilized people to try to ignore the problem altogether, or to insist that it had been much exaggerated, and might, if only it was not so frequently discussed and mentioned, with luck perhaps soon vanish altogether.

This was an attitude which a good many Jews themselves were only too anxious to adopt. The more optimistic 'assimilationists' among them fondly supposed that with the general spread of education and liberal culture the Jews would peacefully melt into their surroundings so that, if the Jewish religion continued to exist, those who practised it would come to be thought of as being neither less nor more different by their Christian fellow citizens than, let us say, Presbyterians or Anglicans or, at the most, Unitarians or Quakers in countries with Roman Catholic majorities. To some degree this process was, in fact, already taking place in the countries of the West; not, to be sure, to a great degree as yet, but from small beginnings great consequences sometimes issued. At any rate, the notion that the Jews were in some sense a nation, as the Italians or, at least, the Armenians were a nation, and had just claims—could, indeed, be conceived as having any claims at all—to a territorial existence as a nation organized in the form of a state, seemed a wild absurdity to the vast majority of those who gave the matter any thought. It was very well for isolated romantics with strong imaginations—Napoleon or Fichte, for example, or the Russian

Decembrist revolutionary Pestel—to suggest that the Jews were in fact a nation though certainly a very odd, scattered one, and should be returned to Palestine, there to create some sort of state of their own. These remained idle fancies which no one, not even their authors, took very seriously. So also later in the century, when benevolent Christians like Laurence Oliphant in England or Ernest Laharanne in France, or Jewish publicists like Salvador or Moses Hess, or the Rabbi Hirsch Kalischer, advocated a return to the Holy Land, this was regarded as mere eccentricity, sometimes dangerous perversity. When novelists—Disraeli or George Eliot—played with romantic nostalgia of this kind, this could be written off as a sophisticated version of the visions of an idealized past that Chateaubriand and Scott and the German romantics had made fashionable— exotic fruit of the new historical imagination, of possible religious or aesthetic or psychological significance, but with no possible relevance to political practice. As for the fact that pious Jews everywhere thrice daily prayed to be returned to Zion, that was, again quite naturally, regarded as an expression of the longing for the coming of the Messiah, for the end of the world of evil and pain, and for the coming of the reign of God on earth, and wholly remote from secular ideas about political self-determination. Even when the growth among the Jews of Eastern Europe of secular education, with the nationalist and socialist ideas which it brought with it, had caused a sufficient ferment among the poorer Russian Jews to cause some of them (especially after the wave of pogroms in Russia that followed the assassination of the Emperor Alexander II) to found small, idealistic, agricultural settlements in Palestine; even after Baron Edmond de Rothschild in Paris had, by a unique act of imaginative generosity, saved these colonies from extinction and made possible a considerable degree of agricultural development; all this still seemed nothing more than a Utopian experiment, queer, noble, moving, but a sentimental gesture rather than real life. When finally the idea of a Jewish state began to be seriously bruited, and reached Western countries, and caught the imagination of such serious and effective statesmen as Joseph Chamberlain and Milner, and when it stirred the enthusiasm of so temperate, sagacious and deeply responsible a man as Herbert Samuel, need we be surprised that some solid and respectable Western Jews could scarcely credit this? The most characteristic reaction was that of Samuel's political colleague and kinsman, Edwin Montagu, at that time himself a member of Mr Asquith's (and subsequently Mr Lloyd George's) Cabinets, who felt personally traduced. The late Lord Norwich once told me that Montagu used to address his colleagues with anger and indignation, declaring that the Jews did not wish—and did not think they deserved—to be sent back to the ghetto; and buttonholed his friends in various drawing-rooms in London, and asked them vehemently whether they regarded him as an Oriental alien and wanted to see him 'repatriated' to the Eastern Mediterranean. Other sober and public spirited British Jews felt no less upset and bitter; similar feelings were expressed in corresponding circles in Paris and Berlin.[1] All this is perfectly intelligible in terms of the life led by the Jews of the Western world, even of the great twentieth century Jewish settlement in the United States. Whatever the truth about the status of the Jews in these countries—whether one was to call them a race, a religion, a community, a national minority, or invent some unique term to cover their anomalous attributes, a new nation and state could not be constructed out of them; neither they nor their leaders conceived this as a real possibility; and this remains true of them still. For, despite all the social friction, discomfort, even humiliation and, in bad times, persecution that they have had to suffer—they were and are, by and large, too

[1] 'To be a Zionist it is not perhaps absolutely necessary to be slightly mad,' Dr Weizmann is reported to have said, 'but it helps.'

[11]

deeply involved in the life of the societies of which they form a part, and have in the process lost too great a part of their original, undiluted national personality to have retained the will to build a totally new life on new foundations. Even Hitler's onslaught did not seem to stir within the majority of the German Jews a feeling of specific Jewish nationalism, but mainly bewilderment, indignation, horror, individual heroism or despair. Jewish nationalism was given reality almost entirely by the Jews of the Russian Empire and to some degree of the Moslem East.[1]

Assimilation, integration, Russification, Polonization had, of course, to some degree also occurred among the Jews of Russia and Poland. Nevertheless the bulk of them lived under their own dispensation. Herded by the Russian Government into the so-called Pale of Settlement, bound by their own traditional religious and social organization, they constituted a kind of survival of medieval society, in which the secular and the sacred were not divided, as they had been (at any rate since the Renaissance) among the middle and upper classes in Western Europe. Speaking their own language, largely isolated

[1] This was predicted almost a hundred years ago with unparalleled prescience by Moses Hess in his most remarkable book, *Rome and Jerusalem*, to this day the most telling analysis and indictment of 'emancipated' Jewish society.

from the surrounding peasant population, trading with them, but confined within their own world by a wall of reciprocal distrust and suspicion, this vast Jewish community formed a geographically continuous *enclave*, that inevitably developed its own institutions, and thereby, as time went on, came to resemble more and more an authentic national minority settled upon its own ancestral soil. There are times when imagination is stronger than so-called objective reality. Subjective feeling plays a great part in communal development, and the Yiddish speaking Jews of the Russian Empire came to feel themselves a coherent ethnic group: anomalous indeed, subject to unheard-of persecution, remote from the alien world in which their lives were cast, but simply in virtue of the fact that they were densely congregated within the same relatively small territory, tending to resemble, say, the Armenians in Turkey: a recognizably separate, semi-national community. In their involuntary confinement they developed a certain independence of outlook, and the problems which affected and sometimes tormented many of their co-religionists in the West—in particular the central question of their status—were not crucial for them. The Jews of Germany, Austria, Hungary, France, America, England, tended to ask themselves whether they were Jews, and if so, in what sense, and what this entailed; whether the view of them by the surrounding population was correct or false, just or unjust, and, if distorted, whether any steps could be taken to correct it without too much damage to their own self-esteem; whether they should 'appease' and assimilate at the risk of losing their identity, and perhaps of the guilt that comes of the feeling of having 'betrayed' their ancestral values; or, on the contrary, resist at the risk of incurring unpopularity and even persecution. These problems affected the Russian Jews to a far smaller degree, relatively secure as they were—morally and psychologically—within their own vast, insulated ghetto. Their imprisonment, for all the economic, cultural and social injustice and poverty that it entailed, brought with it one immense advantage—namely that the spirit of the inmates remained unbroken, and that they were not as powerfully tempted to seek escape by adopting false positions as their socially more exposed and precariously established brethren without. The majority of the Jews of Russia and Poland lived in conditions of squalor and oppression, but they did not feel outcast or rootless; their relations with each other and with the outside world suffered from no systematic ambivalence. They were what they were; they might dislike their condition, they might seek to escape from it, or revolt against it, but they did not deceive themselves or others, nor did they make efforts to conceal from themselves their own most characteristic attributes that were patent to all—particularly their neighbours—to see. Their moral and spiritual integrity was greater than that of their more prosperous and civilized, and altogether grander brothers in the West; their lives were bound up with religious observance, and their minds and hearts were filled with the images and symbolism of Jewish history and religion to a degree scarcely intelligible in Western Europe since the waning of the Middle Ages.

When Herzl with his magnificent appearance and visionary gaze appeared like a prophet from a distant land, many of them were dazzled by the very strangeness and distance which divided them from this Messianic messenger from another world, who could not speak to them in their own language—a remoteness which made him and his message all the more magical and magnetic. But when their leader appeared prepared to accept the compromise solution, offered by the British Colonial Secretary, Mr Joseph Chamberlain, of a settlement in Uganda in place of the unattainable Palestine, many of them were shocked and alienated. Herzl's talent for heroic over-simplification is one that fanatics, possessed by a single idea, often exhibit: indeed it is one of the qualities that makes them exceptionally, dangerously effective, and Herzl ignored difficulties, cut Gordian knots, electrified his Jewish masses in Eastern Europe, developed his ideas before politicians and important personages in the Western world with logic, simplicity, imagination and great fire. The Jewish masses followed him uncomprehending, but aware that here at last was a path towards the light. Like many visionaries Herzl understood issues but not human beings: least of all the culture and feelings of his devoted Eastern European followers. Paris was surely worth a mass: the Jewish problem was urgent and desperate: he was prepared for the sake of a concrete territory waiting for immigration, to disregard, at least for the time being, the saturation of Jewish thought and feeling with the image and symbol of Zion and Palestine, its preoccupation, its obsession by the actual words of the Prayer Book and the Bible. Never has any people lived so much by the written word: not to have realized the crucial importance of this was a measure of the distance of the West from the East. The Russian Zionist leaders did not require to be taught this truth: they grew up with it, and took it for granted. The prospect of nationhood without the land which was the oldest root, the only goal of all their faith, was virtually meaningless for most of them; it could be accepted only by the more rational, but more exhausted—the thinner blooded—Jews of the West, who in any case were not the stuff from which a new society could be moulded overnight. If the Jews of Russia had not existed, neither the case for, nor the possibility of realizing, Zionism could have arisen in any serious form.

There is a sense in which no social problem arose for the Jews so long as rigid religious orthodoxy insulated them from the external world. Until then, poor, downtrodden and oppressed as they might be, and clinging to each other for warmth and shelter, the Jews of Eastern Europe put all their faith in God and concentrated all their hope either upon individual salvation—immortality in the sight of God—or upon the coming of the Messiah whose approach no worldly force could accelerate or retard. It was when this great frozen mass began to melt, that the social and political problem arose. Once the enlightenment—secular learning and the possibility of a freer mode of life—began at first to seep, and then to flood, into the Jewish townlets and villages of the Pale, that a generation grew up no longer content to sit by the waters of Babylon and sing the songs of Zion in exile. Some, in search of a wider life, renounced the religion of their fathers and became baptised and earned positions of eminence and distinction in Russian society. Some did so in Western Europe. Some believed that the injustice done to their people was only a part of the larger injustice constituted by Czarist despotism, or by the capitalist system, and became radicals, or socialists, or members of other social movements, which claimed that the peculiar anomalies of the Jewish situation would disappear as part of the general solution of all political and economic problems. Some among these radicals and socialists and believers in 'Russification' or 'Europeanization' desired the total dissolution of the Jews as a closely knit group among their neighbours. Others, infected by the 'populism' of that time (an idealistic movement of the 'conscience-stricken' sons and daughters of the Russian gentry, seeking to improve the lot of the peasants), conceived in vague and sentimental terms of semi-autonomous Jewish communities, speaking their own Yiddish language and creating in it works of art and science, as one among a family of free communities, constituting, between them, some kind of decentralized, semi-socialist, free federation of peoples within the Russian Empire. Again there were those who, still faithful to the ancient religion, were resolved to keep out the menace of secularism by raising the walls of the ghetto still higher, and devoted themselves with an even more rigid and fanatical faith to the preservation of every jot and tittle of Jewish law and tradition, viewing all Western movements—whether nationalist or socialist, conservative or radical—with equal detestation or horror. But the vast majority of the younger generation of the Russian Jews in the 'eighties and 'nineties joined none of these movements. Affected and, indeed, fascinated by the general ideas then afloat they might be; but they remained *bourgeois* Jews, semi-emancipated from the shackles of their fathers, aware of—discontented by, but not ashamed of—their anomalous status, with a mild but uninhibited devotion to the traditional ways of life in which they were brought up, neither conscious heretics, nor in the least degree renegades, neither zealots nor reformers, but normal human beings, irked by their legal and social inferiority, seeking to lead the most natural and unbroken lives that they could, without worrying overmuch about ultimate ends or fundamental principles. They were devoted to their families, to their traditional culture, their professional pursuits. Faced with persecution, they preserved their closely knit social texture (often by means of bizarre subterfuges and stratagems) with astonishing optimism, tenacity, skill and even gaiety, in circumstances of unexampled difficulty. To this generation, and to this solid milieu, Dr Weizmann belonged, and he became its fullest, most gifted, and most effective representative. When he spoke, it was to these people, whom he knew best, that his words were addressed; to the end of his days he was happiest among them. When he thought of the Jews, he thought of them; his language was theirs, and their view of life was his. Out of them he created the foundations of the new state, and it is their character, ideals, habits, way of life that have, more than any other single set of factors, imposed themselves on the state of Israel. For this reason, it is perhaps the most faithful nineteenth-century democracy at present extant in the modern world.

Dr Chaim Weizmann was born and bred in a completely Jewish milieu near the city of Pinsk, in Western Russia. His father was a timber merchant of small means, a typical member of a lively and devout community, and developed in his many children his own energetic and hopeful attitude to life; in particular, respect for education, for fully formed personality, for solid achievement in every sphere, together with a clear-eyed, concrete—and, at times, irreverent—approach to all issues, combined with a belief that with effort, honesty, faith and a critical faculty, a good life can be lived on earth. Realism, optimism, self-confidence, admiration for human achievement, and above all an insatiable appetite for life as such, whatever it might bring, accompanied by the conviction that all that comes (or nearly all) can, late or soon, be turned to positive advantage—this vigorously extroverted attitude, rooted in a sense of belonging to the unbroken historical continuity of Jewish tradition, as something too strong to be dissolved or abolished by either man or circumstance—these are the characteristics most prominent, it seems to me, in the outlook of this most constructive man whom I wish to describe to you. He was, moreover, of a monolithic solidity of character, incapable of self-pity and self-deception, and absolutely fearless. There is no evidence that he was ever prey to agonizing doubts about moral or political issues. The traditional framework in which he was born was too secure.

Early in life he accepted the proposition that the ills of the Jews were caused principally by the abnormality of their social situation; and that so long as they remained everywhere a semi-helot population, relegated to an inferior and dependent status, which produced in them the virtues and vices of slaves, their neuroses, both individual and collective, were not curable. Some might bear this fate with dignity, others were broken by it, or betrayed their principles and played false roles because they found the burden too heavy. Personal integrity and strength were not enough: unless their social and political position was somehow altered—made normal—brought into line with that of other peoples, the vast majority of Jews would remain permanently liable to become morally and socially crippled, objects of compassion to the kindly, and of deep distaste to the fastidious. For this there was no remedy save a revolution—a total social transformation—a mass emancipation.

Others had reached this conclusion before him: indeed it formed the substance of the most celebrated of all the pre-Zionist pamphlets—Leo Pinsker's *Auto-Emancipation*—and animated the colonizing efforts of the early pioneers of the settlement in Palestine. Herzl translated it into Western terms and gave it coherent and eloquent political shape. Weizmann was not an intellectual innovator: his originality lay in the exceptionally convincing, wholly concrete content which he poured into ideas he received from others. His political, no less than his scientific, genius lay in applied, not in pure, theory. Like his contemporary Lenin, he translated doctrine into reality, and like him he transformed both. But unlike Lenin, he had a harmonious nature, free from that streak of bigoted rationalism which breeds belief in final solutions for which no price—in terms of human suffering and death—can be too high. He was above all things an empiricist, who looked on ideas primarily as tools of practical judgment, and he was endowed with a very strong and vivid sense of reality and the allied faculty of historical imagination—that is to say, with an almost infallible sense of what cannot be true, of what cannot be done.

Weizmann and his generation assumed without question that if Jews were to be emancipated, they must live in freedom in their own land, that there alone they would no longer be compelled to extort elementary human rights by that repellent mixture of constant cunning, obsequiousness and occasional arrogance, which is forced on all dependants and clients and slaves; and finally that this land must—could only—be Palestine. In his milieu scarcely anyone who was convinced of the main thesis seriously conceived of other possibilities. Spiritual ties rightly seemed to them more real than any other; economic and political factors appeared less decisive by comparison. If a people has lived and survived against unbelievable odds by purely ideal resources, material considerations will not, for good or ill, divert it from its vision. At the centre of this vision was the Holy Land. Herzl, Israel Zangwill, others who were born or bred in the West, might need convincing of this: in Russia it was taken for granted by most of those who accepted the fundamental premiss—that the Jews could neither assimilate and melt away, nor remain segregated. If this was sound, the rest followed.

Dr Weizmann shared other unspoken assumptions with his milieu: he was not troubled by the problem of what the government of the future state would or should be: whether, for example, it should be religious or secular, socialist or bourgeois. His notions of justice, equality, communal organization, were non-sectarian and pre-Marxist; he was no more concerned to graft on to his simple, moderate, instinctive, democratic nationalism

[24]

this or that precisely formulated political or social doctrine than were Garibaldi or Kossuth or other great nineteenth-century nationalist leaders, who believed in, and promoted, the renaissance of their peoples not as a policy founded on a particular doctrine, but as a movement which they accepted naturally and without question. Such men—from Moses to Mr Nehru—create or lead movements primarily because, finding themselves naturally bound up with the aspirations of their society, and passionately convinced of the injustice of the order by which they are kept down, they know themselves to be stronger, more imaginative, more effective fighters against it than the majority of their fellow victims. Such men are not, as a rule, theorists: they are sometimes doctrinaire, but more often adapt current ideas to their needs. Little that Dr Weizmann believed throughout his life came to him from books, from the beliefs of this or that social or political teacher, or from any other source than the community that he knew best, from its common stock of ideas, from the very air that he breathed. In this sense, if in no other, he was a very true representative of his people. All his life he instinctively recoiled from *outré* or extremist tendencies within his own movement. He was one of those human beings who (as someone once said of an eminent Russian critic) stood near the centre of the consciousness of his people, and not on its periphery; his ideas and his feelings were, as it were, naturally attuned to the often unspoken, but always central, hopes, fears, modes of feeling of the vast majority of the Jewish masses, with which he felt himself, all his life, in deep and complete natural sympathy. His genius largely consisted in making articulate, and finding avenues for the realization of, these aspirations and longings; and that without exaggerating them in any direction, or forcing them into a preconceived social or political scheme, or driving them towards some privately conceived goal of his own, but always along the grain. For this reason, although he was not a great popular orator, practised no false humility, often behaved in a detached, ironical and contemptuous fashion, was proud, imperious, impatient, and an utterly independent commander of his troops, without the least inclination to demagogy, or talent for it, he never, despite all this, lost the confidence of the vast majority of his people. He was not sentimental, said biting and unpopular things, and addressed himself always to the reason and never to the passions. In spite of this, the masses instinctively felt that he understood them, knew what was in their hearts, and wanted this himself. They trusted and, therefore, followed him. They trusted him because he seemed to them an excep-

tionally powerful, self-confident, solid cham-
pion of their deepest interests. Moreover he
was both fearless and understanding. He
understood their past and their present, but
above all was not frightened of the future.
This last quality is rare enough anywhere;
but is, for obvious reasons, particularly seldom found among the crushed and the oppressed. Like the other great leaders of demo-
cracies in our time, like Lloyd George and the
two Roosevelts, Weizmann had an uncon-
querable belief that whatever the future
brought could be made grist to his, and his
people's, mill. He never abandoned hope, he
remained balanced, confident, representative. He never disappeared from the view of
his followers into private fantasies or ego-
maniacal dreams. He was a man of immense
natural authority, dignity and strength. He
was calm, paternal, imperturbable, certain of
himself. He never drifted with the current.
He was always in control. He accepted full
responsibility. He was indifferent to praise
and blame. He possessed tact and charm to a
degree exceeded by no statesman of modern
days. But what held the Jewish masses to him
until the very last phase of his long life, was
not possession of these qualities alone, dazz-
ling as they were, but the fact that although
outwardly he had become an eminent Western scientist (which made him financially
and therefore politically independent), and

mingled easily with the remote and unapproachable masters of the Western world, his fundamental personality and outlook remained unchanged. His language, his images, his turns of phrase were rooted in Jewish tradition and piety and learning. His tastes, his physical movements, the manner in which he walked and stood, got up and sat down, his gestures, the features of his exceedingly expressive face, and above all his tone of voice, the accent, the inflexion, the extraordinary variety of his humour, were identical with theirs—were their own. In this sense he was flesh of their flesh, a man of the people. He knew this. But, in his dealings with his own people he behaved without any self-consciousness. He did not exaggerate or play up even his own characteristics. He was not an actor. He dramatized neither himself nor his interlocutors. He cultivated no idiosyncrasies. His unshakeable authority derived from his natural qualities, from his combination of creative and critical power, his self control, his calm, from the fact that he was a man of wide horizons, obsessed by nothing, not even his own ideals, and therefore never blinded by passion or prejudice to any relevant factor in his own Jewish world. The failures of the Zionist movement—and they were many—did not embitter him; its successes did not drive him into unrealistic assessments. He combined an acute and highly ironical awareness of the shortcomings and absurdities of the Jewish character—it was a subject on which he was seldom silent—with a devoted affection for it, and a determination at all costs to rescue his people from the humiliating or perilous predicaments in which it landed them. To this end he directed all his extraordinary resource. He believed in long-term strategy; he distrusted improvisation; he was a master of manoeuvre, but despite all that his critics have alleged, he was not in the least machiavellian. He was not prepared to justify wrongdoing by appeals to historical or political necessity. He did not attempt to save his people by violence or cunning—to beat them into shape, if need be with the utmost brutality, like Lenin, or to deceive them for their own good, like Bismarck, or turn their heads with promises of blessings awaiting them in some remote future which could be shaped to anyone's fantasy. He never called upon the Jews to make terrible sacrifices, or offer their lives, or commit crimes, or condone the crimes of others, for the sake of some felicity to be realized at some unspecified date, as the Marxists did; nor did he play upon their feelings unscrupulously, or try deliberately to exacerbate them against this or that real, or imaginary, enemy, as extremists in his own movement have frequently tried to do. He wished to make his nation free and happy,[1] but not at the price of sinning against any human value in which he and they believed. He wished to lead them out of exile into a land where they could live a life worthy of human beings, without betraying their own ideals or trampling on those of others. Like Cavour, whom politically he much resembled in his hatred of violence and his reliance on words as his sole political weapons, he was prepared to use every possible stratagem, to expend his immense charm upon cajoling this or that British or American statesman, or cardinal, or millionaire, into providing the means he needed for his ends. He was prepared to conceal facts, to work in secret, to fascinate, and enslave, individuals, to use his personal followers, or anyone who appeared to him to be useful, as a means for limited ends—only to lose all interest in them, to their bewildered indignation (which was at times exceedingly articulate and bitter), once the need for them was at an end. But he was not prepared to compromise with his own central moral and political principles, and never did so. He was not afraid of making enemies, nor of public or private opinion, nor, in the least

[1] Hermann Cohen, the philosopher, is said to have remarked, with the scorn of an old stoic sage, to Franz Rosenzweig, who tried to convince him of the merits of Zionism, 'Oho! so the gang now wants to be happy, does it?' Weizmann wanted exactly that; he could not see why this was thought a shameful act of surrender.

degree, of the judgment of posterity. He understood human beings and took interest in them; he enjoyed his power of casting his spell over them; he liked political flirtation; he was, indeed in addition to his gifts as a statesman, a political virtuoso of the highest, most inspired, order. These qualities carried their defects with them. They entailed a certain disregard for the wills and attitudes—perhaps rights—of others. He was at times too little concerned with the purposes and characters of those with whom he did not sympathize, and they complained of neglect or heartless exploitation or despotism. He was, in a sense, too fearless, he was too confident that his cause and his friends must triumph, and often underestimated the violence and sincerity of the convictions held by his opponents, both in his own party and in the world at large. This was both a strength and a weakness; it added immeasurably to his feeling of inner security and his optimism, and it liberated his creative energies; but it blinded him to the effects of the fears and the implacable hostility he was bound to encounter among those men outside his own community whom Zionism offended or upset—anti-semites open and concealed, Arabs and their champions, British Government officials, churchmen of many faiths, the respectable and established in general. It seemed a necessary element in his positive,

unswerving, vigorous, almost too uncom-
promisingly constructive temper, to ignore
individual human weaknesses—envy, fear,
prejudice, vanity, small acts of cowardice or
spite or treachery, in particular obstructive
tactics on the part of the feeble, or stupid, or
timid, or ill disposed officials, which more,
perhaps, than major decisions, cumulatively
blocked his path, and, in the end, as everyone
knows, led to bloodshed.

Similarly he tended to ignore his opponents and enemies, personal and ideological.
These he had in plenty, not least in his own
nation. The fanatically religious Jews saw him
as an impious would-be usurper of the position of the Divine Messiah. Tremulous Jews
in important positions in Western countries,
especially those prosperous or prominent
figures who had at last attained to what they
conceived as secure positions in modern
society, achieved after much wandering and
at great expense, regarded him as a dangerous trouble maker likely to open wounds
that they had taken much trouble to bandage
and conceal; at best they treated him with
nervous respect, as a highly compromising
ally. Socialists, radicals, internationalists of
many hues—but especially of course the
Marxists—regarded him as a reactionary
nineteenth-century nationalist, seeking to
lead the Jews back from the broad and sun-
lit uplands of the world-wide society of their

dreams, to the stifling confines of a petty little nationality exiled to a backward region of the Eastern Mediterranean—a grotesque anachronism destined to be swept aside by the inexorable impersonal forces of history. Then there were the Jewish populists in Russia or America who believed in a kind of local or regional Jewish popular culture—a kind of quasi-nationality in exile—Yiddish-speaking, plebeian, unpolitical, a parody of the Russian populism of the time. These looked on Weizmann as a snob, a calculating politician, an enemy to their programmes of warm-hearted social welfare, embellished by amiable and unpretentious arts and crafts and the preservation of carefully protected centres of old-fashioned Jewish life in an unsympathetic and unsentimental Gentile world. And finally there were sceptics and scoffers, sane and ironical, or bitter and cynical, who looked on Zionism as nothing but a foolish dream. He paid little attention to his opponents; but he felt sure that he knew what was strong and what was weak in them—as they did not—and felt sufficiently superior to them morally and intellectually to be determined to save them from themselves (humility, as I said before, was not one of his characteristics). He did not hate them as they hated him—save only the Communists, whom all his life he genuinely feared and detested as swarms of political locusts who, whatever their professions, always destroyed far more than they created. So far as he took notice of them at all, he looked on his opponents as so many sheep that he must attempt to rescue from the inevitable slaughter towards which they seemed to be moving with such fatal eagerness. Consequently he regarded the Russian Socialist leaders, with whom he used to argue (and, at least once, before the First World War, formally debated in a public hall in Switzerland) simply as so many rival fishers of souls, likely to detach from the movement for Jewish liberation and drive to their doom some of the ablest and most constructively minded sons of his people. It is a pity that these debates[1] are not extant. Never can two movements have come into sharper or more articulate collision than in these acrimonious and uniquely interesting controversies between the leaders of the two conceptions of life destined to divide the modern world—communism and nationalism. It is an historical irony that this crucial debate was conducted on the small and obscure platform of the specifically Jewish needs and issues of the time.

[1] Plekhanov, Lenin, Trotsky are the names that, to the best of my recollection, he mentioned to me as being among those who debated against him in Berne and elsewhere at this time. I do not know whether any record of this has been found.

Dr Weizmann believed that he would win —he never doubted this—not because of any overwhelming faith in his own powers, great though these were; not from naïvety—although, in some respects, he did possess the deep simplicity and trustfulness of a certain type of great man, especially in his dealings with Englishmen—but because he was convinced that the tendencies in Jewish life which he represented were central and indestructible, while the case of his opponents was built on the shifting sands of history, rested on smaller areas of experience, and arose out of issues more personal and factional, and therefore ephemeral, than the great, over-mastering, human desire for individual liberty, national equality, and a tolerable life that he felt that he himself represented. He derived great moral strength from his belief in the central ends, the deepest interests, of mankind, that could not for ever be thwarted, that alone justified and guaranteed the ultimate success of great and revolutionary undertakings. He did not, I am sure, distinguish his personal sentiments from the values for which he stood, the historical position that he felt himself to occupy.

When biographers came to consider his disagreements with the founder of the movement, Theodor Herzl, his duels with Justice Louis Brandeis, and with the leader of the extreme right wing Zionists, Vladimir Jabotinsky; or, for that matter, his differences with such genuine supporters of his own moderate policies as Sokolov, or Ben Gurion, and many a lesser figure, they will—they inevitably must—ask how much of this was due to personal ambition, love of power, underestimation of opponents, impatient autocracy of temper; and how much was principle, devotion to ideas, rational conviction of what was right or expedient. When this question is posed, I do not believe that it will find any very clear answer: perhaps no answer at all. For in his case, as in that of virtually every statesman, personal motives were inextricably connected with—at the lowest—conceptions of political expediency and, at the highest, a pure and disinterested public ideal. Weizmann committed none of those enormities for which men of action, and later their biographers, claim justification, on the ground of what is called *raison d'état*—the notorious reasons of state which permit politicians caught in some major crisis to sacrifice the accepted standards and principles of private morality to the superior claims of state, or society, or church, or party. Dr Weizmann, despite his reputation as a master of *Realpolitik*, forged no telegrams, massacred no minorities, executed and incarcerated no political opponents. When Jewish terrorism broke out in Palestine he felt and behaved much as

Russian liberals did when reactionary Czarist ministers were assassinated by idealistic revolutionaries. He did not support it; in private he condemned it very vehemently. But he did not think it morally decent to denounce either the acts or their perpetrators in public. He genuinely detested violence: and he was too civilized and too humane to believe in its efficacy, mistakenly perhaps. But he did not propose to speak out against acts, criminal as he thought them, which sprang from the tormented minds of men driven to desperation, and ready to give up their lives to save their brothers from what, he and they were equally convinced, was a betrayal and a destruction cynically prepared for them by the foreign offices of the Western powers. Mr Bevin's Palestine policy had finally caused Weizmann to wonder whether his own lifelong admiration for, and loyalty to, England and British Governments had perhaps cost his people too dear. His devotion to his cause was deeper than to any personal issue. And since he was neither vain, nor constitutionally obstinate, he was not blinded to the possibility of error on his own part. He did not literally give up hope; he believed that it would take more than ministers and civil servants to defeat the Jewish settlement fighting for its very survival. He kept saying about the Foreign and Colonial Offices, as he paced up and down his hotel room in London, and listened to reports about this or that post-war anti-Zionist move by Whitehall, 'It is too late. It will not help them.' But he wondered whether his own earlier trust in England had not gratuitously lengthened the birth-pangs of the new Jewish state. He was not convinced that a Jewish state might not be premature; he would have preferred Dominion status. The Peel Commission's partition scheme of 1936 had marked the highest point of fruitful collaboration between the British Government and himself, and he regarded those who had wrecked this scheme, especially in the Foreign Office, as responsible for the calamities that followed. He knew that he had himself been removed from his office because he trusted these men too much. But his own life-long reputation as an anglophile, as a moderate, as a statesman, was now to him as nothing in the face of the struggle for life of the Jewish settlement in Palestine. He had moments of black pessimism; but he believed that men fighting in a just cause must, when the worst came to the worst, sell their lives as dearly as possible—if need be, like Samson in the temple of the Philistines. And he held this to be no less true for nations than individuals.

When the Arab-Jewish war broke out his conscience was clear. He was not a pacifist, and the war was—no Jew doubted this—one of self-defence. All his life he believed in, and practised, a policy of accommodation; he had politically suffered for it, and the war wasnot one of his making.

Like the late Mr Justice Holmes, Weizmann had all his life believed that when great public issues are joined one must above all take sides; whatever one did, one must not remain neutral or uncommitted, one must always—as an absolute duty—identify oneself with some living force in the world, and take part in the world's affairs with all the risk of blame and misrepresentation and misunderstanding of one's motives and character which this almost invariably entails. Consequently in the Jewish war of independence he called for no compromise, and he denounced those who did. He regarded with contempt the withdrawal from life on the part of those to whom their personal integrity, or peace of mind, or purity of ideal, mattered more than the work upon which they were engaged and to which they were committed, the artistic, or scientific, or social, or political, or purely personal enterprises in which all men are willy-nilly involved. He did not condone the abandonment of ultimate principles before the claims of expediency or of anything else; but political monasticism—a search for some private cave of Adullam to avoid being disappointed or tarnished, the taking up of consciously utopian or politically impossible positions, in order to remain true to some inner voice, or some unbreakable principle too pure for the wicked public world—that seemed to him a mixture of weakness and self-conceit, foolish and despicable. He did not disguise his lack of respect for purists of this type. He did not always treat them fairly; and his point of view is one which has, of course, been opposed, and indeed detested, by men of the greatest courage and integrity; but I should be less than candid if I did not confess that it is a point of view that seems to me superior to its opposite. However that may be, it was of a piece with all that he believed and was.

Weizmann lived a rich inner life, but he did not escape into it to avoid the second best realities of the outside universe. He loved the external world. He loved whatever seemed to him likely to contribute to a broad, full, generous tide of life in which the full resources of individuals could be developed to their richest and most diversified extent. Best of all he liked positive human gifts: intelligence, imagination, beauty, strength, generosity, steadfastness, integrity of character, and especially nobility of style, that inner elegance and natural breadth and sweep and confidence which only old and stable cultures, free from calculation, narrowness and neurotic self-preoccupation, seemed to him to possess. England seemed to him to display these

qualities most richly, and he remained devoted to her until the end of his days. This
fidelity, which was not unreciprocated, at
first sustained, and then broke, his political
life. He loved her independence, freedom,
dignity, style. These were free men's virtues,
and them, above all, he desired the Jews to
acquire and develop and possess.

The connection of England with the
Zionist experiment, and in particular with
Weizmann's part in the securing of the
Balfour declaration and the mandate over
Palestine, is usually regarded as a somewhat
fortuitous one. It is sometimes asserted that
had he not happened to obtain a post in the
University of Manchester, he might never
have settled in England, and would then
scarcely have met Arthur Balfour in the early
years of the century, and, in that case, would
certainly have been in no position to influence
either him or Lloyd George or any of the
other British statesmen whose voice was decisive in the establishment of the Jewish
settlement. This is true, and is, perhaps, a
characteristic case of the influence of accident in history. And then one may begin to
wonder if it is altogether an accident that it
was to England that Weizmann migrated
from the continent of Europe. For to him, as
to so many Jews of his background and up-
bringing in East Europe, England, above all
other lands, stood for settled democracy,

humane and peaceful civilization, civil liberty, legal equality, stability, toleration, respect for individual rights, and a religious tradition founded as much on the Old Testament as the New. She embodied all those free middle-class virtues that made for anglomania in France in the last century of the *ancien régime*, and in eastern Europe for much the same reasons, in the nineteenth century. It was, above all, a country in which the Jews enjoyed a secure and peaceful and progressive existence, in full possession of the rights of men and citizens—everything, in short, that the more educated among them craved for most of all, and lacked most deeply in their own midst. This was the atmosphere in which Dr Weizmann was brought up, and he therefore arrived in England with a preconceived respect bred in him by the attitude of his entire milieu.[1] His long and fascinated flirtation with Lord Balfour, from which so much in his life and that of the Zionist movement sprang, is not intelligible unless it is realized that in Balfour he met what, at all times, he found most attractive:

[1] It is a significant fact that in a letter written in Hebrew before he was twelve to his former schoolmaster, he speaks of England as the good and free country which will help the Jews to establish their own state. I owe this fascinating piece of information to Mr Boris Guriel of Rehovot, who has done so much to preserve the record of Weizmann's life and activity.

aristocratic attributes in their finest and most fastidious form.

Weizmann was a celebrated and, indeed, when he set himself to it, an irresistible political seducer, but he did not offer himself except to those whom he truly admired, and he was not prepared to enter into a personal relationship for the sake of mere political expediency with those who morally or politically—and, at times indeed, aesthetically—repelled him. Perhaps he would have been wiser not to quarrel with Mr Justice Brandeis, not to despair of 'building a bridge between Pinsk and Washington'; nor to ignore Arab leaders, or dignitaries of the Roman Church; nor to react so strongly to the brutal ill-humour of the late Mr Ernest Bevin; but he could not break his own temperament. He liked only large, imaginative and generous natures, and he believed that the future of his people was bound up with what they alone could give, that agreement could be reached only with such men, and that marriages of pure political convenience were bound to fail. His opponents condemned this as mere romanticism, mistakenly as I believe. He believed that lasting agreement required a large measure of genuine harmony of interests, principles and outlook between negotiators, and came to believe that this affinity obtained between the Jews and the English to a unique degree. This last, like most generalizations of this type, may have been a sentimental error, and one for which both sides have paid dearly, but it was an interesting and attractive error, and one that deeply influenced the character of the new state. Perhaps Weizmann was carried away too far by his personal tastes. He liked the English almost too well: he liked the concreteness of English life, language, ideals; the moderation, the civilized disdain of extremes, the whole tone of public life, the lack of cruelty, of excitement, of shoddiness. He liked still more the wayward imagination, the love of the odd and the idiosyncratic, the taste for eccentricity, the quality of independence. He was a great charmer as Disraeli had been before him; and the English like to be charmed. They might be conscious, as Queen Victoria perhaps knew when Disraeli wrote or spoke to her, that they were being enticed; but they were not—until their bad days—suspicious of it; they did not think that the power to delight, the play of fancy, gay and often mordant humour, bold ideas moderately expressed, political romanticism conveyed in a mixture of vivid similes, sober, temperate language, and perpetual reference to intelligible material achievement, were necessarily insincere or wicked, or constituted a danger to themselves. They were secure themselves and, therefore, they were courteous; they listened, and they welcomed opportunities of being fascinated. No French statesman, no American (not to speak of the Germans whom Herzl tried to address), would have let himself to be as deeply and, above all, so willingly influenced by Weizmann's political imagination and historical memories, as Balfour or Lloyd George or Churchill, and many a soldier, many a politician and professor and journalist, gladly allowed themselves to be. They were not merely beguiled by a clever and delightful talker; the values of the foreign chemist and his English hosts did in fact largely coincide. They did not find it difficult to think of the world in the terms in which he spoke, or at any rate were quite ready to see it so, and were grateful to anyone who lifted them to that level. And in fact they were right, and those who dismissed his talk as full of cunning or deliberate exoticism were morally and politically unperceptive. For it turned out that history conformed to Dr Weizmann's vision, compounded of hard-headed common sense and deep historical emotion, and not to the normal categories of the 'realists' in the government departments of England, France and the United States. What he advocated was nearly always practicable. What his opponents urged was for the most part falsified by events.

I have said that his words were addressed

D

to reason rather than feeling. His method of argument was, as a rule, neither a demonstration founded on statistical or other carefully documented evidence, nor emotional rhetoric, nor a sermon addressed to the passions; it consisted in painting a very vivid, detailed, coherent, concrete picture of a given situation or course of events; and his interlocutors, as a rule, felt that this picture, in fact, coincided with reality and conformed to their own experience of what men and events were like, of what had happened, or might happen, or, on the contrary, could not happen; of what could and what could not be done. The moral, historical, economic, social and personal factors were blended in Weizmann's remarkable, unrecorded expositions much as they combine in life (this he spoke most effectively face to face, in private, and not before an audience). He was not an analytic, but a synthetic thinker, and presented a pattern or amalgam of elements, not the essence of each separate component isolated, taken apart, and looked at by itself. There was no country in which such concreteness was a more habitual form of thought than England, and the natural sympathy which his mode of thought and action found here caused him to invest—invest irretrievably —far more of his emotional capital in his friendship for England than, I think, he realized. And an element in the opposition to him and to his ideas whether by his own followers, or from outside his movement, derived from the instinctive revulsion to English values on the part of those who found themselves in greater sympathy with other outlooks or forms of life.

You must forgive me if I revert again to the theme of his passion for England; it is very central in him, and in his ideal, for he wanted the new Jewish society—the new state —to be a political child of English—almost exclusively English—experience. He valued especially the tendency toward instinctive compromise, whereby sharp edges are not indeed planed away, but largely ignored by both sides in a dispute if they threaten to disrupt the social texture too widely, and break down the minimum conditions for common life. Moreover he believed profoundly in the application of scientific method to human life, in which England once led the world; his interest in pure science was very limited; but he was a magnificent inventor, and wanted invention to respond to basic human needs and create new, more civilized ones—he believed in the unlimited transforming powers of natural science. This was at the heart of his optimism, of his hope and faith in the future; and he liked to think of this view as characteristically British. It was therefore one of the bitterest disappointments of his life when, in the later thirties, and during the last war, his services as a scientist were virtually ignored by the British Government departments. When war broke out in 1939, he offered to lay aside some of his political preoccupations, in order once more to try to be of service to his adopted country, as he had been with his celebrated invention in the First World War. He met with lack of response. He complained of dullness, timidity, pettiness, conservatism, fear of the future, on the part of most of the British officials with whom he discussed these matters, of their total inability to grasp the economic position of their country, still less the dangers and opportunities in the world that was bound to come. Throughout the war he reverted to this fact with melancholy incredulity; he found it difficult to accept that as a scientist, he had, in fact, met with a far readier response in America. He wondered whether British imagination and appetite for life were dying. It seemed to him that one and the same negative attitude—a symptom of exhaustion and defeat—was palpably present in the fears of the new world and the desperate attempts to cling to an outworn conception of a world political order that he found in Whitehall, and in the squalid efforts to back out of British commitments to the Jews in Palestine. It all seemed to him part and parcel of the general retreat from moral and political principles, beginning with the condoning of Arab

violence in Palestine, Japanese aggression in
Manchuria, of Mussolini in Abyssinia, of
Franco in Spain, and, above all, of course, of
Hitler. And when, speaking of anti-Zionists,
he said to the Prime Minister, Mr Churchill,
in 1940 or 1941, with characteristic bold-
ness, 'Remember, sir, our enemies are also
yours', this is certainly part of what he
meant. Political appeasement, weakness,
nervous fears, blindness to distasteful facts,
seemed to him merely an aspect of one and
the same gloomy condition of decline, which
blinded the eyes of British economic plan-
ners to the possibility—to the necessity,
indeed—of recouping the slipping British
position by one of the main devices which,
he felt sure, could still help to save it—
the imaginative application of the resources
of the African empire to the creation of a
great new synthetic materials industry; it was
a field about which he himself, as a chemist,
knew a great deal, and one he had done
much to develop. Since he thought in vast,
synoptic terms, he saw the Jewish establishment in Palestine in these same scientific
terms. As he reflected on the poverty of
the land and its lack of natural resources, he
placed his hope upon turning the one kind
of capital that the Jews did seem to possess—
technical skills, ingenuity, energy, desperation—to the production of miracles in scientific technology, that would contribute to the

building of the new world, and especially the new, post-Chamberlain Britain. He believed that the British would understand this, and was depressed by finding that this seemed no longer so. He felt rebuffed, he no longer recognized the nation he had loved so steadfastly and disinterestedly.

He felt he had a right to complain. On the two principal occasions when he suffered public defeat at the hands of his own followers, the principal cause of it lay in what seemed to them his fanatical reliance on the good faith of British Governments. He was compelled to resign in 1931 as a protest against the policy of concessions to Arab violence at the expense of its victims, begun by the Labour Government with the Passfield White Paper, and continued by its successors. In 1946 a very similar situation once again arose; and it could plausibly be argued that Weizmann's policy of accommodation with Britain, which had led to a total betrayal of the Jewish position in 1938–9, must, if persisted in (he was then advocating acceptance of what was called the Morrison Plan), lead to a further series of promises broken and hopes destroyed. In the end he began, with painful reluctance, to think that this might be true. He could not bring himself to admit this publicly; but in private he spoke with bitter scorn about what seemed to him the complacent stupidity of post-Churchillian statesmanship. When some of his English friends (Lord Keynes for example) tried to say to him that England was too tired and too poor to carry the burden of its incompatible promises to the Jews and the Arabs any longer, and consequently must abandon both parties to their own devices, he rejected this doctrine with scorn and fury, as craven, unworthy of the men who urged it, and above all a false analysis and a suicidal policy for any great power.

His own position became increasingly unenviable. His followers in Palestine and elsewhere looked on his anglophile policy as bankrupt, and on him as too deeply committed to it—and with it to a world that had vanished—to be anything but a dignified but obsolete mammoth of an earlier age. No member of the government in England or America was anxious to see him. He was a tragic, formidable and politically embarrassing figure. It had always been a somewhat daunting, not to say punishing, experience both for ministers and their officials to meet the full impact of Weizmann's terrifying indignation. This was now no longer necessary. The relief was almost audible. The Colonial Office treated him with icy politeness. He was systematically snubbed by the Foreign Office, as often as not by a junior official, who took their cue from their superiors, or perhaps felt that they could with impunity allow their own solidly pro-Arab sentiments free expression. He was treated with brutal rudeness by Mr Bevin, who conceived for him, and for the entire Zionist movement, a notorious personal hostility which nothing staunched. And yet he could not give up his oldest political love. England meant more to him than all other countries put together. When I stayed with him in Palestine, as it still was, in 1947, during the height of Jewish military and terrorist activity against the British forces stationed in that country, his fondness for, and delight in seeing, the British commander of his district and other British officers, continued unabated, to the mounting scandal of his followers. He felt betrayed, and he could not, despite all his realism and his tough-minded approach to politics, understand what had happened. The romantic, somewhat Churchillian, image of England as moved, in the last resort, by her moral imagination, and not by a short view of her self-interest or passing emotion, would not leave him. The England which had stood alone against barbarism and evil, the England for which his son had lost his life, was scarcely less real to him than his vision of the Jewish past and future. He tried to close his eyes. He fell back on his scientific work. He often said that nothing had a morally more purifying effect, after the unavoidable contaminations of public life, than the impersonal work of a researcher in his laboratory where the truth could not be cheated, and the vices and follies of men played little part. He busied himself in his work in the Institute[1] at Rehovot that bears his name. But the remedy was not wholly effective. He had put his faith in British statesmen and had rendered his followers into their hands; every shipload of immigrants turned away by Mr Bevin and Sir Harold McMichael brought his part in the betrayal home to him. From it he never fully recovered.

The British Government—in particular the Labour Government—had wounded him as no one else ever could; least of all the Jews. He did not ask, and did not expect, gratitude from his own people. The fate of Moses seemed to him natural and perhaps deserved. To his own close followers he seemed, if anything, altogether too invulnerable: especially when he behaved toward them (as he often did) with casual offhandedness, or ill-concealed contempt, or, from time to time, the sudden ruthlessness of a great man of action. Yet their personal loyalty

[1] The Institute was the deepest love of his old age. He always spoke of it, and of all his colleagues and, indeed, everyone connected with its work, with immense personal pride and affection, and derived from it a feeling of satisfaction that nothing else gave him to an equal degree. The flourishing state of this great establishment is evidence of the lasting vitality that he communicated to all that he truly believed in.

survived most of the shocks which he administered. For his personal magnetism was quite unique. Men crossed great distances to visit him, knowing or suspecting that he had completely forgotten why he had sent for them, and that when they arrived he would be genuinely puzzled by their appearance, at best agreeably surprised, and would dismiss them with a few careless, gay and friendly sentences. His relationship to his immediate followers was, in some ways, not unlike that of Parnell to the Irish party in the House of Commons. And they treated him with much the same mixture of adoration, nervous respect, resentment, worship, envy, pride, irritation, and, almost always, in the end, the overwhelming realization that before them stood someone of more than human size, a powerful, sometimes terrifying, leader of newly liberated prisoners in terms of whose thoughts and activities their own history was largely made. They might revolt, but in the end they always—most of them—submitted to the force of his intellect and personality.

It was otherwise with England. His preoccupation—it grew at times to an obsession (perhaps his only *idée fixe*)—with Anglo-Zionist relations blinded him to too many other factors in the situation—the attitude of other powers, especially in Europe, of the Arab rulers, of social and political forces within the Palestine settlement itself. The collapse of the Anglo-Zionist connection was not only intertwined for him with his own personal failure to retain real power in the movement that was his life; it also seemed to support the claims of those who said that against Britain only violence paid—that nothing would save the Jewish settlement but methods of terrorism—a view that he abhorred and rejected passionately with his whole being, then, and all his life. But there was something far more at stake than even that. He could not bear the thought that the state that he had desired to establish, and which he desired to place under the protection of Great Britain, would now perhaps never acquire those moral and political attributes which he had so long and steadfastly admired as peculiarly English and which, he now gloomily began to wonder, were disappearing everywhere—even from this island where he had spent his happiest years.

He was in due course elected President of the State of Israel, a position of splendid symbolic value, but little power. He accepted it, fully realizing what it meant and what it did not mean, amid the acclamation of Jews and their well-wishers everywhere. He understood the extent of his own achievement and never spoke of it; he was one of those rare human beings who estimate themselves at their true worth, and see themselves in the true perspective in which they see others. His autobiography, particularly in its earlier chapters, is an astonishingly objective and life-like narrative, without a trace of dramatization, exaggeration, vanity, self-pity, self-justification; it conveys his authentic, richly and evenly developed, autonomous, proud, firmly built, somewhat ironical nature, free from inner conflict, in deep, instinctive harmony with the forces of nature and society, and therefore possessed of natural wisdom, dignity and authority. His unhappiness came from without, hardly ever from within; he remained inwardly tranquil to the end of his days. He knew well that his achievement was without parallel. He knew that, unlike any man in modern history, he had created a nation and a state out of the flotsam and jetsam of the diaspora, and had lived to see it develop an independent, unpredictable life of its own. This worried him. Freedom and independence were not enough. Like the ancient prophet that western statesmen sometimes saw in him, he craved for virtue. He disliked certain elements in Jewish life, and wondered uneasily whether they would emerge uppermost. Obsessed and lop-sided natures repelled him, he was contemptuous of addiction to doctrine and theory without constant concrete contact with empirical reality. He did not value the achievements of the unaided intellect for their own sake, and admired them only when they made some contribution to human life. He liked solidity, practical judgment, vitality, gaiety, understanding of life, dependability, courage, stoutness of heart, practical achievement. Martyrs, failures, casualties, victims of circumstance or of their own absurdities—the stock subjects of the mocking, sceptical Jewish humour—filled him with distress and disgust. The central purpose of the entire Zionist experiment, the settlement in Palestine, was designed to cure the Jews of precisely these wounds and neuroses that only their enforced rootlessness had bred in them. He therefore particularly disliked the mixture of *avant-garde* sophistication, political fanaticism, cynicism, vulgarity, cleverness, *humeur-noir*, knowingness and occasional bitter insight with which able, typically Central European, Jewish journalists were filling the pages of the world's press. Even more he hated stupidity, and he did not trouble to conceal this. In his last years, when he was living in peace and great honour in his home in Rehovot, a figure respected by the entire world, he was occasionally haunted by nightmare visions of the future of the state of Israel. He saw it jeopardized by just such a combination of stupidity—innocent, fearless, but blind—with the corrupt and destructive cleverness of slaves, the aimless, feckless, nihilistic restlessness inherited from too long a sojourn in the ghetto. Yet he also saw that this might not happen; and then the thought that the dream had come true against all the overwhelming odds of his youth and man-hood, that he was actually living among Jews, a free nation in their own country, would fill him with incredible happiness.

He was not a religiously orthodox Jew, but he lived the full life of a Jew. He had no love for clericalism, but he possessed an affec-tionate familiarity with every detail of rich, traditional life of the devout and observant Jewish communities, as it was lived in his childhood, in the villages and small towns of eastern Europe. I cannot speak of his reli-gious beliefs; I can only testify to his pro-found natural piety. I was present on more than one occasion, towards the end of his life, when he celebrated the *Seder* service of the Passover with a moving dignity and nobility, like the Jewish patriarch that he had become. In this sense he had always lived in close con-tact with the life of the Jewish masses, and his optimism had its source in the belief which they shared—that their cause was just, their sufferings could not last for ever, that some-where on earth a corner must exist, in which their claim to human rights—their deepest desires and hopes—would find satisfaction at last. Neither he nor they would accept the proposition that the mass of mankind could remain for ever indifferent to the cry for justice and equality even on the part of the weakest and most wretched minority on earth. Men must themselves work and fight to secure their basic rights. This was the first prerequisite. Then, if these claims were recognized as valid in the great court of justice that was the public conscience of mankind, they would, soon or late, obtain their due. Neither force nor cunning could help. Only faith and work, founded on real needs. 'Miracles do happen,' he said to me once, 'but one has to work very hard for them.' He believed that he would succeed—he never doubted it—because he felt the pressure of millions behind him. He believed that what so many desired so passionately and so justifiably, could not for ever be denied; that moral force, if it was competently organized, always defeated mere material power. It was this serene and absolute conviction that made it possible for him to create the strange illusion among the statesmen of the world that he was himself a world statesman, representing a government in exile, behind which stood a large, coherent, powerful, articulate community. Nothing was —in the literal sense—less true, and both sides knew it well. And yet both sides behaved—negotiated—as if it were true, as if they were equals. If he did not cause the embarrassment that suppliants so often engender, it was because he was very dignified, and quite free. He could be very intimidating; he uttered, in his day, some very memorable insults. Ministers were known to shrink nervously from the mere prospect of an approaching visit of this formidable emissary of a non-existent power, because they feared that the interview might prove altogether too much of a moral experience: and that, no matter how well briefed by their officials, they would end, for reasons which they themselves could not subsequently explain or understand, by making some crucial concession to their inexorable guest. But whatever the nature of the extraordinary magic that he exercised, the one element signally absent from it was pathos. Dr Chaim Weizmann was the first totally free Jew of the modern world, and the state of Israel was constructed, whether or not it knows it, in his image. No man has ever had a comparable monument built to him in his own lifetime. I truly envy the task of his biographers.

DATE DUE